# Finding Out About
# TUDOR LAW AND ORDER

# Madeline Jones

B.T. Batsford Limited, *London*

# Contents

**Cover illustrations**

The colour illustration is from *The Statutes of England* (Bodleian Library, Oxford); the black and white print on the left shows traitors' heads on London Bridge (Mansell Collection); "A Caveat or Warning" is taken from A.V. Judges, ed., *Elizabethan Underworld*, Routledge and Kegal Paul, 1930 (print: Central Library, Bromley).

**Frontispiece**

Whipping a vagabond.

Typeset by Tek-Art Ltd, Kent
and printed in Great Britain by
R J Acford
Chichester, Sussex
for the publishers
B.T. Batsford Limited,
4 Fitzhardinge Street
London W1H 0AH

ISBN 0 7134 5048 7

## ACKNOWLEDGMENTS

The Author and Publishers would like to thank the following for permission to reproduce illustrations: BBC Hulton Picture Library for page 41; Bodleian Library, Oxford for pages 19 (left) and 37; British Museum for pages 9, 20, 29 and 42; Cassell & Co. (and Oxfordshire County Libraries) for page 38; Coventry Corporation for page 23; Essex County Council for page 30; Ipswich Museum Committee for page 5; Mansell Collection for pages 3, 4, 6, 8, 13, 14 and 25; Routledge and Kegan Paul (and Central Library Bromley) for pages 27, 32 and 36; Mrs Jennifer Ruby for page 19 (right); B.A. Seaby for page 18. The illustration on page 21 is Crown copyright. The photograph on page 47 was taken by the Author. The map on page 44 was drawn by R.F. Brien.

The Author would like to give her special thanks to the staff of the Bodleian Library and to Elizabeth Phillips for research assistance.

# Introduction

In 1485 the first Tudor ruler, Henry VII, won his crown in battle. Many people must have wondered how long he would keep it. Since the 1450s there had been many battles between rival groups of nobles wanting to control the king or to put a new king on the throne. In fact, Henry VII and his successors (his son Henry VIII and grandchildren Edward VI, Mary and Elizabeth) kept the crown firmly on their heads. However, as you will see, there were some rebellions against them, and no Tudor ruler felt completely secure. This made them treat rivals and suspected plotters harshly.

After Henry VIII quarrelled with the Pope and broke away from the Roman Catholic church in the 1530s, religious disputes increased tension. There were fears, too, of local risings, especially if times were hard and food ran short. In 1566, for example, four Essex men announced:

> **We can get no work nor we have no money, and if we should steal we should be hanged, and if we should ask, no man would give us, but we will have a remedy one of these days, or else we will lose all, for the commons [ordinary people] will rise, we know not how soon, for we look for it every hour. Then will up two or three thousand in Colchester and about Colchester ... for there is no more to do but one to ride on a horse with a clap and cry "They are up, they are up!," and another to ring "Awake!", for ye shall see the hottest harvest that ever was in England.**

The four were tried and hanged for this seditious talk.

For ordinary people, it was important to have a ruler strong enough to keep peace and order, to prevent powerful men from terrorizing their neighbourhoods and to supervise local magistrates. It was not easy for even the most determined ruler to do these things. There was no paid, professional police force or regular army. Communications were bad: it took at least two days for a messenger, riding hard, to take news or an order from London to York or to Plymouth. Criminals could often escape justice. An Elizabethan writer, William Harrison, praised the English custom of raising a "hue and cry" – that is, getting the parish constable to organize a search if anyone was robbed or attacked, and, if that failed, to pass the news on from village to village. In practice, though, Harrison added:

> **thieves have been let pass, because the covetous and greedy parishioners would neither take the pains nor be at the charge, to carry them to prison, if it were far off; [and] when hue and cry have been made even to the faces of some constables, they have said "God restore your loss! I have other business at this time."**

*The heads of executed traitors were displayed in public places – these are shown on the entrance to London Bridge.*

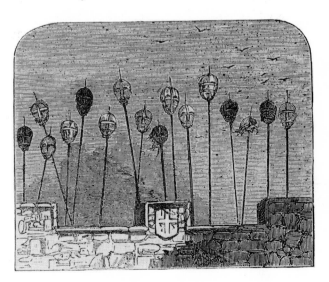

Partly because it was difficult to catch criminals or to prevent crime, punishments were very severe for those who were caught – if they were found guilty. It was local men on the jury who decided if an accused person was innocent or guilty. In the 1590s at least one J.P. complained that country people hesitated even to accuse thieves because "they would not procure a man's death for all the goods in the world".

Sympathy was not always shown to offenders, though. Crowds jeered at people in the stocks or even on their way to execution. Ordinary people became accustomed to seeing brutal sights. John Stow, a Londoner, actually saw a man executed just outside his own door. In this book you will find many incidents like this to remind you how different life was in Tudor times from life today. However, you may also find some things which remind you of modern problems, so, as you read this book, be on the alert both for differences and for similarities. Remember, too, that we can only include a sample of all the material there is on this topic. You will be able to find more for yourselves.

*A Tudor view of the Tower of London (1550) by Wyndegaard. The Tower was used as a prison for important people.*

PEOPLE TO ASK
The librarian at your local public library will be able to help you find books, old maps, etc. Go to the Reference section, or the Local History section if there is one. If you have a local museum the curator there may also be able to help.

1. VISUAL SOURCES
a) *Maps* Old (or sometimes even modern) maps of your area are very useful in showing buildings like an old court house or place names telling you where a stocks or even a gallows once stood (in Ludlow in Shropshire there is an area still known as Gallows Bank).

b) *Pictures* As well as pictures produced in the Tudor period, like those you can find in this book, later drawings or paintings of local scenes sometimes show an old stocks or a town gaol which has now disappeared. Ask in your local library or museum.

c) *Objects* You can find stocks preserved in various places – in the Cotswolds at Stow-on-the-Wold, for example. These are not likely to date from the Tudor period (you can work out why if you think what material they were made of and what happens to that material left out in all weathers), but they will be of the same pattern. In museums you may find examples of other means of punishment, like a ducking-stool.

WRITTEN SOURCES
You will find that you need to use printed versions of Tudor written records. Tudor handwriting is very difficult to read, though you can have some fun puzzling out short pieces (try to get some photostat copies from your library that you can work on at home). Tudor spelling, too, is very different from modern spelling, and there is little punctuation. In this book, both spelling and punctuation have been modernized to make the extracts easier to understand.

a) *Records of local law-courts* Some sets of records for the courts of Quarter Sessions, held in each county by the J.P.s, have been published – and translated from the Latin in which they were originally written. Some records of manorial courts (see page 40) have also been published. Ask your local librarian if there are any in your library, or try the nearest County Record Office in your county town (write beforehand to the County Archivist for an appointment).

b) *Town records* Many town council minutes of meetings and account books have been published in whole or in part – you will find plenty of examples in this book. These contain interesting details about law and order. Again, ask your librarian what is available in your area.

c) *Tudor pamphlets* Some collections of these have been published, and they are very entertaining. You will find some listed on page 47, and your local public library may be able to order them for you if they are not in stock.

d) *Books by Tudor authors* There are modern reprints of some very useful Tudor accounts of the methods and problems of keeping order. Some are listed on page 47. You will probably find John Stow's *Survey of London*, published in 1598, in your library, and you can use the Index to look up prisons like Newgate to see what he says about them. You will find the language a little difficult at first, so it is a good idea to work with a friend, and to have a teacher nearby to ask should you get into difficulty.

*This splendid example of a Tudor ducking- (or cucking- ) stool is in Ipswich Museum. Can you make out the date? You will find out more about the punishment of ducking on page 41.*

5

# Rebellion

Tudor people remembered the Wars of the Roses of the fifteenth century. They were ready to listen when their rulers reminded them of the disorder and danger that rebellion brought. There were a number of rebellions against the Tudors, but they were unsuccessful. No Tudor monarch lost his or her throne, or even had to give way to rebel demands (though they sometimes pretended to for a time, until the rebels could be defeated).

## PREACHING THE DUTY OF OBEDIENCE

Clergymen helped to convince ordinary people that it was a sin to rebel:

> . . . Take away kings, princes, rulers, magistrates, judges, and such states of God's order, no man shall ride or go by the highway unrobbed, no man shall sleep in his own house or bed unkilled, no man shall keep his wife, children and possessions in quietness . . . we may not in any wise [in any way] resist violently or rebel against rulers . . . . But we must . . . patiently suffer all wrongs or injuries, referring the judgment of our cause only to God . . . . Let us all therefore fear the most detestable vice of rebellion . . . ("A Homily on Obedience", 1547, quoted in G.R. Elton, *The Tudor Constitution*, 1960)

Why might people in 1547 be especially worried about possible rebellion? (If you don't already know what was special about the king at that time, look at the picture.)

## "MOST TRUE AND LAWFUL SUBJECTS"

Even the rebels proclaimed their loyalty to their ruler. Poor people often thought that if the ruler knew their grievances he or she would help them. Powerful rebels also avoided blaming the ruler for anything that was wrong: you can find out from the next extract whom they blamed instead.

> Thomas, Earl of Northumberland and Charles, Earl of Westmoreland, the Queen's most true and lawful subjects . . . to all her highness' people, sendeth greeting: Whereas divers new set-up nobles about the Queen's Majesty have and do daily not only go about to overthrow and put down the ancient nobility of this realm, but also have

Edward VI was only nine when he became king in ▷ 1547. He could not rule for himself and his advisers soon started to quarrel with each other.

misused the Queen's Majesty's own person, and also have by the space of twelve years now past, set up and maintained a new-found religion and heresy, contrary to God's word .... As you tender [love] ... your country ... come and resort unto us with all speed, with all such armour ... as you or any of you have. This fail you not herein ... God save the Queen. (The Proclamation of the Earls, 1569, quoted in Anthony Fletcher, *Tudor Rebellions*, Longman, 1968)

Elizabeth I was not softened towards these rebels in the North by these loyal declarations. When her troops defeated them, she ordered hundreds of executions. The Earl of Northumberland himself was beheaded at York in 1572 (the Earl of Westmoreland escaped abroad). Can you work out which religion these rebels supported? (Use the Date List on page 46 to help you.)

## TROUBLE IN NORFOLK, 1549

Local grievances, especially over enclosure of common land, led to a rebellion in Norfolk in July and August 1549. About 16,000 men are said to have joined Kett, the rebel leader. You can see from the account written by the brother of a man who opposed the rebels why some local people would have welcomed Kett's defeat.

... the gentlemen they [the rebels] took they brought to the Tree of Reformation [at their camp near Norwich] to be seen of the people to demand what they would do with them; where some cried hang him, and some kill him, and some that heard no word cried even as the rest ... and indeed they did press their weapons to kill some of those gentlemen

## NORWICH SUFFERS FROM BOTH SIDES, 1549

Kett and his followers captured Norwich, government troops later recaptured it. The rebels then tried to re-enter the city.

... certain [rebels] coming over the water did set divers houses in South Confort on fire where was burned a whole parish or two on both sides the way with much corn and merchantries [goods] and stuffe ...

After this, because many soldiers had not been lodged nor housed a good space, was every man's house appointed to receive a company; the better to make them hearty went many to their beds and had victuals [food] furnished which encouraged them much .... (Nicholas Sotherton, *The Commoyson in Norfolk 1549*)

About 3000 rebels were killed before, in or after the final battle with government troops on 27 August. Fifty, including Kett, were tried and executed for treason – some "hanged in the cross of the market" in Norwich, wrote Sotherton. Write a letter from a Norwich citizen after the rebellion, giving your account.

brought to them which they did of such malice that one Master Wharton, being guarded with a lane of men on both sides from the said tree into the city, they pricked him with their spears and other weapons ... Nicholas Sotherton, *The Commoyson in Norfolk, 1549* (written in the 1550s)

(Notice that the rebels threatened, but did not actually harm, their prisoners.)

Why is it useful to know that this description was written by someone unsympathetic to the rebels?

# Treason

Treason – anything that threatened the king or queen – was the most serious crime of all. It was savagely punished.

## A TRAITOR'S DEATH

Ordinary people convicted of treason were hanged, drawn and quartered (that is, they were cut down while still alive from the gallows and their bodies were then mutilated). Crowds gathered to watch this horrible spectacle, and accounts of the traitors' crimes and death were often published.

> **The several Confessions of Thomas Norton and Christopher Norton, two of the Northern Rebels, who suffered at Tyburn, and were drawn, hanged and quartered for Treason, May 27, 1570. Imprinted at London . . .**
>
> **. . . and afterwards their heads [were] set on London Bridge, and their quarters [limbs] set upon sundry gates of the city of London, for an example to all Traitors and Rebels, for committing High-Treason against God and their prince . . .** (*State Trials*, 1570)

*Torture was used to make suspects confess or reveal their accomplices. This picture show the rack being used in the Tower of London. You can see the victim's arms and legs being stretched.*

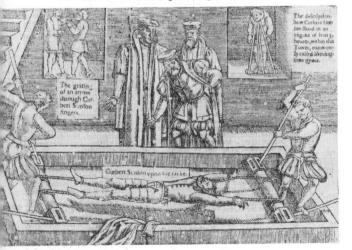

## TORTURE

Those suspected of treason were sometimes tortured to make them confess and reveal the names of anyone else involved. A Roman Catholic priest, Father Gerard, survived to tell of his experiences in the Tower of London in 1597. Unlike the man shown in the picture, Gerard was not put on the rack, but in the "manacles" – that is, he was hung up by his hands.

> **All the blood in my body seemed to rush up into my hands and arms: I thought that blood was oozing out from the ends of my fingers . . . but it was only a sensation caused by my flesh swelling above the irons holding them . . .**
> (Gerard's *Autobiography*, quoted in A.L. Rowse, *The Tower of London in the History of the Nation*, Weidenfeld and Nicolson, 1972)

## THE EXECUTION OF THE DUKE OF NORFOLK, 1572

Noblemen convicted of treason were allowed an easier death. They were beheaded, often on Tower Hill in London. The first to die there in Elizabeth I's reign was the Duke of Norfolk, who had been involved in a plot against the Queen. On the scaffold, he protested his loyalty and asked the Queen's forgiveness. Then he shook hands with those around him,

> **. . . desiring them to pray for him; amongst the rest, the Executioner did on his knees desire forgiveness of his death, who did very courteously forgive him, and put into the hand of the Executioner four sovereigns [coins] of gold and eighteen shillings and sixpence of silver. This done, the Duke**

It was very dangerous even to be suspected of treason. Torture was used to gain information, and anyone tried for that crime had little chance of being acquitted. This was not surprising, as those accused were given no help in defending themselves. They were not allowed to have lawyers to speak for them. They were not even given copies of the charges against them – they only heard these read in court. You can see from the following extract how one defendant failed in an attempt to get permission to make notes during his trial:

> **Then said Abington, I beseech your honours that I may have a pair of writing tables to set down what is alleged against me, that I may yield a sufficient Answer thereunto.**
> **Sandes [the Clerk of the Crown]: It was never the course [custom] here.**
> **Sir Christopher Hatton [one of the royal councillors appointed to try the case]: When you hear anything you are desirous to answer, you shall speak an Answer at full, which is better than a pair of tables.** (*State Trials*, 1586 – Edward Abington)

The Jury found Abington guilty of taking part in Babington's plot (see page 12) and he was condemned to death. If you were on trial for your life, why might you find it helpful to have a written copy of the accusations against you?

Why, do you think, were Tudor governments (and many ordinary people, too) so harsh to traitors or suspected traitors?

*People of high rank found guilty of treason were beheaded. This sketch shows the arrangements made for the execution of Mary Queen of Scots, at Fotheringay Castle (Northampton) in 1587.*

> **kneeling down . . . he made his prayers to God . . . . Then he arose up and pulled off his velvet gown, his black satin doublet, and his velvet night-cap, and gave them to the Executioner . . . and so kneeling at the block, he laid down himself, and rose again, and laid the straw and other things in such sort, as he might in a more convenient manner yield himself for the speedier execution . . . . The Duke yielding himself to the block, refusing to have any handkerchief before his eyes, his head was at one chop cut off, and showed to all the people . . .** (*State Trials*, 1571)

Why was it a good idea for the victim to give a generous present to the executioner, do you think?

Riots easily flared up in Tudor times, especially when food or work was scarce. If speedy action was not taken against the rioters, a great deal of damage could be done.

## SERIOUS TROUBLE IN LONDON, 1517

London craftsmen found themselves competing for customers with foreign workers who had settled in the city and with traders from abroad. Complaints against "strangers" were followed by trouble in the streets. You can see from the account given by Holinshed how the riot developed:

> **On the eight and twentieth day of April, divers [various] young men of the city picked quarrels to certain strangers [foreigners] as they passed by the streets, some they did strike, some they buffeted, and some they threw into the kennel [ditch]; wherefore the mayor sent some of the Englishmen to prison . . . . Then suddenly rose a secret rumour, and no man could tell how it began, that on May day next the city would rebel and slay all aliens, insomuch that divers strangers fled out of the city . . .**

A curfew was imposed on the eve of May Day, to last until 9 a.m. on 1 May. An alderman, Sir John Mundie, tried to enforce this:

> **. . . Sir John Mundie . . . found two young men in Cheape playing at the bucklers [having a mock fight] and a great many of young men looking on . . . he commanded them to leave off. And for that [because] one of them asked why, he would have had him to the**

> **Counter [prison]. Then all the young prentices [apprentices] stepped to, and resisted the alderman, taking the young fellow from him, and cried: prentices and clubs. Then out at every door came clubs and weapons. The alderman fled and was in great danger. Then more people arose out of every quarter . . . and brake up the counters, took out the prisoners that the mayor had thither committed for hurting the strangers . . .**

After the failure of attempts to calm the crowd,

> **. . . they ran headlong into Cornhill and there . . . spoiled divers houses of the Frenchmen . . . from ten or eleven of the clock these riotous people continued in their outrageous doings till about three of the clock, at what time they began to withdraw . . . and by the way they were taken by the mayor and the heads of the city, and sent some to the Tower, some to Newgate, and some to the Counters, to the number of three hundred.**
> (*Holinshed's Chronicles*, 1586-7)

The King's Council sent soldiers into the city, and after trials had been held, 14 of the prisoners were executed, on gallows set up all round the city. The rest were finally pardoned by the King, Henry VIII, but only after being brought with ropes round their necks to beg for mercy.

Can you think why the King and Council were so angry about this riot? (One clue is where it took place – another, who was attacked.) Notice who started the riot. Do you know, or can you find out, their age-group? The name given to this incident was "Ill (or 'Evil') May Day".

## A FOOD RIOT

In the 1590s bad harvests brought food shortages. There were disturbances in many areas, like this one in Somerset described by a local J.P.:

**Others there be . . . that stick not [don't hesitate] to say boldly they must not starve, they will not starve. And this year there assembled eighty in a company, and took a cartload of cheese from one driving it to a fair, and dispersed it amongst them, for which some of them have endured long imprisonment and fine . . . which may grow dangerous by the aid of such numbers [of vagrants] as are abroad, especially in this time of dearth [famine], who no doubt animate them to all contempt both of noblemen and gentlemen, continually buzzing into their ears that the rich men have gotten all into their hands and will starve the poor . . .** (Edward Hext to Burghley, September 1596)

In what way did this J.P. think vagrants were stirring up trouble? What do you think he was afraid the hungry people might do?

## FEAR OF RIOT IN LONDON, 1593

The government's fear of disturbance in London was great enough for it to order cruel treatment of anyone suspected of stirring up trouble. The Queen's Council wrote to the Lord Mayor in 1593:

**Whereas there was a . . . vile ticket or placard set up upon some post in London purporting [suggesting] some determination and intention the apprentices should have to attempt some violence on the strangers [foreigners] . . . . Because oftentimes it doth fall out of such . . . beginnings that further mischief doth ensue if in time it be not wisely prevented, we have thought good to pray your Lordship to cause the person by you apprehended . . . to be strictly and very carefully examined . . . [as to] who were in any way privy to the same and did give him advice or encouragement . . . and [if] he will not by fair means be brought to utter his knowledge, we think it convenient he shall be punished by torture . . . and so compelled to reveal the same . . .** (Acts of the Privy Council, 1592-3)

What kind of "further mischief" would the Council have in mind?

## CONFLICT IN BANBURY, 1600

Quarrels over religion sometimes caused riots. The market cross in Banbury was attacked by a group of townsmen in 1600, because it reminded them of Roman Catholic worship. Other inhabitants then "assembled in manner of a Tumult or Mutiny" to defend it, but the famous "Banbury Cross" was destroyed. It was not rebuilt until the nineteenth century. Its steps had been used by market traders to set out their wares. This was one reason why its destruction was unpopular. Can you think of other possible reasons?

# Plots

Fear of a successful plot to kill the ruler was especially strong in Elizabeth I's reign. Elizabeth was a Protestant and if she died without children the next ruler would be the Catholic Mary Queen of Scots. Though most of Elizabeth's Catholic subjects were perfectly loyal, they were often suspected of plotting. Real plots were discovered from time to time.

## PRECAUTIONS AGAINST PLOTS IN THE NORTH, 1574

The Queen and her Council sent instructions to J.P.'s "in the north parts" to keep a close watch on the discontented in April, 1574 (you can remind yourself why the government was especially nervous about the North by looking at page 7).

> ### Articles to be enquired upon
> . . . that by your discretions . . . you in good and secret sort lay good watch and especially to get knowledge and understanding as well of all meetings, conferences and practices of all persons suspect or known to mislike either of the present state and government for Religion or otherwise, and also of all such as be goers or travellers about with messages, letters, tokens, news or books from or to persons suspect in religion . . . and to take and apprehend all such offenders . . . (Letter from Queen and Council to York, 2 April, 1574, York Civic Records)

Which people were "suspect in religion" at this time from the point of view of the Queen and Council?

## THE BABINGTON PLOT, 1586

Anthony Babington was one of a group of young men who planned to murder Elizabeth and put Mary Queen of Scots on the throne of England. Babington's letter to Mary went straight to Walsingham, who was in charge of Elizabeth's Secret Service and who was intercepting Mary's post. The plotters were arrested in August 1586:

> Ringleaders in this . . . treason were certain gentlemen and others . . . order was taken for a very strict inquiry and search . . . such officers, as upon whom the charge was imposed, demeaned [behaved] themselves so precisely (and specially the constables of London, to their praise be it spoken) that they spared not their next neighbours houses, but . . . did search them, proceeding so far . . . that they went into the very bedchambers of many a wealthy and worshipful person . . .

It took some days to catch all the conspirators: but when all were captured the Londoners rejoiced:

> . . . some wearied themselves with pulling at the bell ropes, which were rung both day and night, as upon the day of her majesty's coronation; . . . others . . . although wood was then at a sore extent of price [expensive], yet they spared not their stacks or piles . . . but brought . . . every house a portion, where fires might conveniently be made and without danger . . . none were more forward herein than the mean [poor] sort of people who . . . being unprovided of fuel, parted with a penny or two to buy a few sticks . . . . And surely infinite was the wood spent . . . as may appear by the number [of bonfires] betwixt Ludgate and Charing Cross . . . above threescore, by count of the writer hereof, who went of purpose to view them . . . (*Holinshed's Chronicles*, 1586-7)

Why would the people have been so keen to light bonfires?

Fourteen of the plotters were executed, and, as a result of her approval of the plot, Mary herself was beheaded in 1587.

## A BABINGTON PLOT BALLAD

Ballads were the popular songs of the day, and they were often composed about events like the discovery of a plot. As well as being sung, they were sold as printed pamphlets, though the printed ones had to be licensed and that meant the government had to approve of them. You can see why this ballad would have had no trouble in gaining a licence.

> Their treasons once discovered,
>   then were the traitors sought:
> Some of them fled into a Wood,
>   where after they were caught,
> And being brought unto the Tower,
>   for joy the bells did ring,
> And throughout London Bonfires made,
>   where people Psalms did sing,
> And set their tables in the streets
>   with meats of every kind,

> Where was prepared all signs of joy
>   that could be had in mind,
> And praised the Lord most heartily,
>   that with his mighty hand
> He had preserved our Gracious Queen
>   and people of this land.

("Ballad on the Babington Plot", quoted by C. Firth, *Ballad History of the Later Tudors, Transactions of the Royal Historical Society*, 1909)

Imagine you were a Protestant, or a secret Catholic, in London in 1586. Write a letter to a friend about the discovery of the Babington Plot. Remember, if you were a Catholic it would be very dangerous to show sympathy for the plotters.

*Babington and his friends are shown here making plans to kill Queen Elizabeth. The Latin reads: "These are my comrades whom perils themselves bring forth."*

# Judges and Justices of the Peace

Royal judges went twice a year from the law-courts in Westminster to each county to try serious criminal cases. These trials were called the Assizes. Rulers also appointed land-owners in each county, and mayors and senior councillors in the towns, as justices of the peace. These local magistrates were supposed to supervise their own areas, to keep the peace there and to punish offenders. It was their duty to see that the laws made in Parliament were carried out locally.

## OXFORD MAKES ARRANGEMENTS FOR THE ASSIZES

The visit of the judges to a town was a big occasion. It was profitable to the citizens, because many visitors came to watch the spectacle, but it also cost the town money;

> **1583, 20 June**
> **It is agreed at this Council that Mr Kyte shall have of this City for the use of his stable on the backside of his house yearly from henceforth, at the assizes . . . for the Judges' horses the sum of 10s at every of the same assizes, and the same stable to be planked and racked at the charges of this city . . .**
>
> **Chamberlain's Accounts, 1583-84**
> **For a gallon of sack (wine) and a gallon of claret wine given to the Judges in Winter Assizes 4s 4d**
> **For 4 pairs of gloves given to them at the same time 13s 4d**
> (*Selections from the Records of the City of Oxford*, ed. W.H. Turner, 1880)

In spite of the entertainment and presents, going on Assize could be dangerous for the judges: in 1577, "both the judges" were on a list of 300 or so people who died "of the poisonous smell of the gaol" (that is, of gaol fever caught from prisoners) at the "Black Assizes" in Oxford.

Tudor judges would have looked much the same as those at the top of this picture, which shows a law-court not long before Henry VII won the crown. Can you see the clerks writing their record of the court's proceedings? If you look carefully, you will see why court records of this period are called "Rolls". (Think of how the long strips of parchment would be stored.)

## JUSTICES OF THE PEACE

Sir Thomas Smith, who wrote a book about the government of England under Elizabeth I, admired the work of the J.P.s. Here he describes some of their powers.

**Each of them hath authority upon complaint to him made of any theft, robbery, manslaughter, murder, violence, complots [plots], riots, unlawful games, or any such disturbance of the peace and quiet of the realm, to commit the persons whom he supposeth offenders to the prison . . . till he and his fellows do meet . . . . These [the J.P.s] do meet four times in the year, that is in each quarter once, to enquire of all the misdemeanours . . .**
(Sir Thomas Smith, *De Republica Anglorum*, 1565)

You can work out from this account why the meetings of the J.P.s in each county were called "Quarter Sessions". As you can see, the J.P.s dealt with many crimes. However, they often left the most serious cases for the judges to try at the Assizes.

## A COMPLAINT ABOUT A JUSTICE OF THE PEACE, 1601

Not all J.P.s were conscientious. Henry VII, in 1489, set up a system whereby "all manner of men, as well the poor as the rich . . . that is hurt or grieved in anything" could complain against a J.P. – first to another J.P.; then, if nothing was done, to the judges at the next Assizes; finally to the King himself, if need be. In 1601, the Lord Chief Justice, a very important judge, contacted Sir Nathaniel Bacon, a Norfolk J.P., about a complaint from a Norfolk gentleman, Emmanuel Callard. Callard said that he and others had

**. . . divers and sundry times made complaint unto one John Kempe of Antingham Esq., one of the Justices of [the] Peace . . . for the suppressing of certain alehouses within the same Town [of Cromer], there being more than is either fit or necessary. And many misdemeanours and abuses offered, and continually committed, [in the alehouses], being supported . . . not only by the said Mr Kempe . . . but also by one Spillman and two others, being constables within the said Town of Cromer . . . and . . . that many unlawful games are there commonly used [and] servants and others thither drawn . . . at undue times . . .** (H.W. Saunders, ed., *The Official Papers of Sir Nathaniel Bacon . . . 1580-1620*, Camden Society, 1915)

As a J.P., John Kempe should have closed down rowdy alehouses. Sir John Popham, the Lord Chief Justice, asked Sir Nathaniel Bacon to look into the matter and report to him.

Notice that this complaint was made by a local gentleman. What might make it more difficult for a poor man to get a hearing for a complaint against a J.P.?

We still have J.P.s today. See if you can discover the names of any in your area and what their duties are. You will notice one big difference from Tudor times: many J.P.s today are women.

# Watchmen and Constables

Tudor constables were not like our police constables today. They were not paid professionals. Instead, they were ordinary villagers or townsmen, sometimes chosen for the job by other members of the local community, sometimes taking their turn to do it just for one year. Watchmen also took turns, sometimes helping the constable, sometimes keeping watch for wrongdoers on their own. You can discover from the extracts whether these jobs were likely to be popular or not.

## THE PROBLEMS OF SERVING AS CONSTABLE

A rhyme made up just after the end of the Tudor period neatly sums up the constable's difficult position:

> **The Justices will set us by the heels**
> **If we do not as we should,**
> **Which if we perform, the townsmen will**
> **    storm,**
> **Some of them hang us if they could.**
> ("The Song of James Gryffon, Constable of Albury", 1626, quoted in F. Aydelotte, *Elizabethan Rogues and Vagabonds*, 1913

*Ale-houses were often centres of noise and disturbance.*

## WOLVERHAMPTON'S INEFFICIENT CONSTABLES

The Staffordshire J.P.s in 1592 had to deal with a complaint against Wolverhampton's constables:

> **Nicholas Allen and William Foster, Constables of Wolverhampton; for not executing their office in punishing of Rogues which the town is greatly charged [burdened] with . . .**
> (*Staffordshire Quarter Sessions Roll 33*

From other sections of this book find out what other jobs constables had to do (the Index will help you).

*Constables were responsible for putting offenders in the stocks.*

## USELESS WATCHMEN

The historian A.L. Rowse discovered a letter from Elizabeth I's chief councillor, Lord Burghley, which shows how inefficient watchmen – and constables,

16

too – could be. It was written when a big search was in progress for men involved in the Babington conspiracy (see page 12).

Sir, as I came from London homeward in my coach, I saw at every town's end the number of ten or twelve standing with long staves, and until I came to Enfield I thought no other of them but that they had stayed for avoiding of the rain, or to drink at some alehouse, for so they did stand under pentices [overhanging roofs] at alehouses. But at Enfield finding a dozen in a plump [group], when there was no rain, I bethought myself that they were appointed as watchmen, for the apprehending of [catching] such as are missing. And thereupon I called some of them to me apart and asked them wherefore they stood there. And one of them answered, 'To take three young men.' And demanding how they should know the persons, 'Marry,' said they, 'one of the parties hath a hooked nose', 'And hath you', quoth I, 'no other mark?' 'No,' saith they. And I asked who appointed them. And they answered one Banks, a head constable, whom I willed to be sent to me . . . these watchmen stand so openly in plumps as no suspected person will come near them . . . (Burghley to Walsingham, August 1586, quoted in A.L. Rowse, *The England of Elizabeth*, 1950)

What do you think Burghley said to the head constable? You can find some good scenes making fun of watchmen like these in Shakespeare's play *Much Ado About Nothing*.

## ABINGDON ORGANIZES THE WATCH, 1584

25 October, 1584
. . . to avoid the danger of fire and misdemeanours . . . it is ordered by the Mayor . . . that yearly from the feast of St Michael Th'archangel, unto the feast of Th'ascension, That two householders dwelling together next adjoining, shall either [watch] in their own persons or else find two sufficient householders to watch for them, which shall be allowed by Mr Mayor nightly by order, And there to watch from eight of the clock in the afternoon, until five of the clock in the morning . . . and those which watch shall give their next neighbour warning to watch the next night following, and then to show themselves to the Mayor or his Deputy at the Cross by eight of the clock as aforesaid, with sufficient weapon for watchmen. (Bromley Challenor, ed., *Selections from the Records of the Borough of Abingdon*, 1898)

Can you work out the time of year to which this order applied? If you were a householder and did not want the job of watchman yourself, what did you have to do?

The following extract tells you *why* a man might not want to be one of the watch (it was not a job given to women).

Item: Thomas Bostocke of Tetnall Regis [is brought before the Staffordshire J.P.s] for that he and others beat and evil entreated the watchmen of Tetnall Regis aforesaid. (*Staffordshire Quarter Sessions Roll* 33)

# Over-Mighty Subjects

Justice was supposed to be provided equally for rich and poor. However, it was possible for the rich and powerful to bully their neighbours or escape the consequences of their own wrongdoing. Tudor rulers knew they had to make themselves, and the law, obeyed. It was dangerous to allow any subject to think that he or she could defy the monarch or show contempt for the law-courts.

## LAWS AGAINST RETAINERS

It was usual for noblemen at the beginning of the Tudor period to have large troops of armed followers. From Henry VII's reign onwards Tudor rulers struggled to have these bands of "retainers" dismissed or at least reduced in number. The Statute of Liveries of 1504 stated:

> **. . . our said sovereign lord the king [Henry VII] ordaineth . . . that no person . . . give any livery [uniform] or sign or retain any person, other than such as he giveth household wages unto [his household servants] . . . and if he do the contrary . . . for every such livery and sign, badge or token . . . 100s [fine] . . .**

Why would retainers be given uniform or a badge to wear? Why would the King be against nobles keeping armed followers? Noblemen went on recruiting bands of followers, but laws like this one meant that the King's Council could pounce on anyone who went too far and make an example of him.

## TOO MUCH INFLUENCE

William Lambarde, who wrote a number of books about the law and the law-courts in Elizabeth I's reign, knew the difficulty of disciplining important local figures:

> **. . . some stick not to use means both forcible and subtle, for the winning of their wills: thinking, that for their apparent Nobility, ancient Gentry, large possessions, overflowing riches or store of Friends (joined with the Rooms [positions] of high Authority, that they have above their neighbours) no passage ought to be fore-closed against them . . .** (William Lambarde, *Archeion*, 1591)

The followers of a nobleman would wear his badge. The Tudor rulers had their own special badges, and encouraged their loyal followers to wear these. You probably know of one Tudor badge – the rose (shown opposite). You may have another in your purse or pocket! This one is called the "portcullis with chains" (see if you can work out what a portcullis is). Some eager courtiers even carved Tudor badges around the doorways of their houses: why do you think they did this?

## THE COURT OF STAR CHAMBER

The Tudors used a special court to deal with "over-mighty subjects". It consisted of the Council and the chief judges. There was no jury. The court usually met in a room with a ceiling painted with stars, which gave it its name. It could not condemn anyone to death, but it could fine or even order physical punishments, like the loss of a hand or ear. Fines were the usual punishment, though. Sir Thomas Smith in 1565 suggested why the court was so effective:

> If . . . riot be complained of, the party [the accused] is sent for, and he must appear in this Star Chamber, where seeing . . . as it were the majesty of the whole realm before him, being never so stout [bold] he will be abashed; and being called to answer (as he must come, of what degree soever he be) he shall be so charged with such gravity . . . of those chief personages of England . . . that, what courage soever he hath, his heart will fall to the ground . . . . For that is the effect of this court, to bridle such stout noblemen or gentlemen which would offer wrong by force to any manner men . . . (Sir Thomas Smith, *De Republica Anglorum*, 1565)

*Lord Burghley on his mule. He was the Crown's representative and a leading figure in the Elizabethan Court of Star Chamber.*

Why would the "stout noblemen" be more frightened by Star Chamber than by any ordinary law-court?

Star Chamber was a popular court under the Tudors, even though it had no jury. Normally the right to trial by jury is looked on as a most important liberty for the subject, but can you think of any ways in which "over-mighty subjects" in Tudor England might put pressure on juries so as to interfere with justice? Remember that at this time jurymen were supposed to come from the same neighbourhood as the person on trial.

*The Tudor rose.*

19

# Wales and the North

Distant parts of the Tudor kingdom were the hardest to control. Wales had its own traditions and a history of family feuds. Scotland was a separate kingdom, and Scots and English raided each other across the border. English rulers needed powerful nobles to defend the Scottish border and act as wardens of the marches ("march" is another word for "border"). However, it was difficult to stop such noblemen fighting each other, or to make them obey orders.

## THE COUNCIL IN THE MARCHES OF WALES

Henry VII sent his son Arthur to govern Wales with the help of a council. This Prince of Wales never became king – he died at Ludlow in 1502. Instead, his brother succeeded as Henry VIII, and in the 1530s he developed a strong council to supervise Wales and its borders. Ludlow Castle served as the prison for those the council punished. Queen Elizabeth sent new Instructions to this council in 1574. See what idea you can get from them about life in Wales at this time.

> **And whereas divers persons in Wales have commonly used [been accustomed] heretofore to go . . . to the church, . . . fairs, markets and other places appointed for justice, in harness [dressed for battle] and privy coats [livery, uniform], the Queen's Highness' pleasure is that from henceforth no man shall wear neither harness nor privy coats neither in churches, fairs markets or any other place of justice, except such as shall be licensed . . . by the Queen's Highness or her honourable Council . . .** (Instructions to the Council of Wales, 1574)

Why was it important to stop armed men coming to "places appointed for justice" – i.e. where law-courts were held?

Ludlow Castle, residence of the President of The Council of Wales and the Marches.

## AN "OVER-MIGHTY SUBJECT" IN WALES

The Council of Wales could not always discipline a powerful man. Sir William Herbert of Swansea was one of the council's own members when, in 1595, during a quarrel with a rival family, his servants released two prisoners from a Cardiff gaol. The Herbert followers then spent

> . . . divers days and weeks after this walking and braving [swaggering] still up and down the streets in great troops and companies both by day and by night, weaponed and armed . . . without check or rebuke . . . (Star Chamber Proceedings, quoted in Penry Williams, *The Council in the Marches of Wales under Elizabeth I*, 1953)

Herbert was reported to the Court of Star Chamber (see page 19) and fined heavily – though he seems to have remained a member of the Council for Wales.

## THE COUNCIL OF THE NORTH

Henry VIII also set up a strong royal council in the North to keep order and act as a law-court. He sent new Instructions to it in the 1540s:

> His Majesty, much desiring the quietness and good governance of the people there, and for speedy and indifferent [impartial] administration of justice, intendeth to continue his right honourable Council called the King's Council in the North Parts . . . . His Majesty . . . ordaineth that his said Council shall by the space of one whole month in the year at least remain at York, by the space of one other month at Newcastle, by the space of one other month at Kingston-upon-Hull, and by the space of one other month at Durham . . . (*Instructions to the Council of the North,* c.1544, quoted in G.R. Elton, *The Tudor Constitution*, 1960)

What advantages were there in moving the council about?

## TAKING PRECAUTIONS

People living near the northern border knew that they might be raided at any time, and not only by the Scots. An official survey of the lands of the Northern rebels of 1569 described the land around Alnwick in Northumberland where the people were

On the Scottish borders landowners lived in tower-houses like this one (Smailholm Tower, near Kelso). In 1548 the family that owned it changed sides, deciding to obey the king of England instead of the king of Scotland. Even at the end of the Tudor period it was wise to have a house you could defend if you lived in the North. An Act of Parliament in 1601 talked of border-people being captured from their houses and "kept barbarously and cruelly until they have been redeemed by great ransoms".

> . . . very poor, because they are able to keep no greater number of cattle of any kind than may lay in house at night, because it is so near Scotland of one part and the thievish country of Tynedale of the other part, whose whole life and delight is only in stealing, robbing and spoiling their poor neighbours and more harm is done to the poor countrymen by the riders of Tynedale than by the open enemies the Scots. (Quoted in A.L. Rowse, *The England of Elizabeth*, 1950)

Look up Tynedale on a detailed map of England. What impression do you get from this extract of life in that area in the Tudor period?

# Order in the Towns

Most Tudor towns were small. Apart from London, only Norwich had a population of more than 10,000 in the 1520s. The important port of Bristol had about 10,000 inhabitants – the number living today in small towns like Bridgnorth in Shropshire or Hexham in Northumberland. Some Tudor towns were still run by the lord of the manor, but others had charters of privileges from the King or Queen, and in these a town council led by a mayor kept order and punished minor criminals.

## RESPECT FOR THE TOWN AUTHORITIES

In small towns, where everyone knew everyone else and thought him or herself as good as anyone else, it was not easy for councillors to get the respect they should have. In Beverley, Yorkshire, the council decided to make a stand in 1578:

> **Orders of the Mayor and Governors**
> **7 November 1578**
> **Thomas Sympson, waterman,**

*The Tudor townhall at Burford is now the town museum. The back part was used as the town gaol in Tudor times*

## THEFT IN SOUTHAMPTON

It was the duty of the mayor to take statements from anyone suspected of a crime in the town.

> **The Examination of John Huggins . . . labourer . . . 14th day of March, 1593 . . . before the mayor . . .**
>
> **Being examined as concerning certain linen [such] as towels and napkins and**

committed to ward [prison] for the space of 8 days for certain opprobrious [insulting] words uttered against the Governors, and then to abide further order . . .
20 November 1578
**Thomas Sympson having been punished by imprisonment and a fine, upon submission made is now set at liberty. He promises to behave himself reverently and obediently . . .**

How long did Thomas Sympson spend in prison?

## THE COSTS OF KEEPING ORDER

Each town bought its own equipment for punishing offenders, as the Account Book of Burford in Oxfordshire records:

> **1586 paid to Mr Alderman, Mr Chadwell and Richard Dalby for the making of the pillory and for a pair of stocks in the same £4.10.5d.**
> **1587 paid to William Symons and John Lyme for repairing of the stocks 5s 6d**
> (R.H. Gretton, ed., *The Burford Records* 1920)

other things taken from hedges in the backside of his neighbours house [such] as Mr Hopkins and others, and supposed to be stolen by him this examinant sayeth that he never did any such matter, neither never used . . . any the backdoors whereof he is charged . . . nor never did take any linen from the hedges or other place. And for a purse showed unto him . . . found in Mr Hopkins garden, saith that it is not any of his purse neither is he acquainted with any such matter. (*Southampton Books of Examinations and Depositions*)

Why did John Huggins' neighbours suspect him of this crime? Thefts of clean washing were common in Tudor times. Where was washing put to dry and how would this make it easy to steal?

## AN ALDERMAN'S HOUSE UNDER ATTACK

Prosperous townsmen could afford luxuries like glass windows in their houses, but these were very vulnerable if anyone wanted to pay off a grudge. In Oxford, the city council often quarrelled with the university, and students were suspected of many crimes. It was thought their tutors either turned a blind eye or actively encouraged them.

<u>Complaints of the City against the University</u>: Item XIX . . . that the first day of March last past, which was Shrove Tuesday [1530] at midnight, there came certain persons and brake a large glass window of William Flemings, Alderman of the Town of Oxford, and within XV nights after at midnight there came the same company or other, and there broke the glass of another window of X lights painted

*Walled towns could, and did, shut their gates to keep trouble out. In 1553 Coventry, one of whose gates is shown here, "caused the Common bell to be rung and the Gates shut and Walls manned" against the Duke of Northumberland, who was trying to make Lady Jane Grey Queen instead of Mary Tudor.*

with birds . . . (W.H. Turner, ed., *Selections from the Records of the City of Oxford*, 1880.)

The council suspected that servants of the proctors, the officers of the university who were supposed to keep students in order, were involved in this affair. The university replied indignantly that "where any offences be done, it chanceth more oftener the townsmen to be transgressors than the scholars to be the occasion thereof . . ."

If you live in or near an old town, or if you visit one, see if you can find out where the prison or "cage" was in Tudor times – the local library or museum may be able to help you. You may be able to discover where the stocks and pillory were, too.

# London

London was the only really large town in Tudor England. By the 1520s there were already about 60,000 inhabitants, and by 1603 as many as 200,000. Many of the newcomers to the growing city were poor people hoping for work or charity. Some Londoners took to crime. Thieves flourished in the crowds, and catching them was difficult in the maze of narrow streets. London apprentices, too, were easily persuaded to fight and riot (you will have read about one London riot on page 10).

### "A GREAT CORRUPTION OF YOUTH"

London's mayor and aldermen found it a struggle to keep order in and around the city. They felt that places of amusement attracted undersirables. No theatres were allowed in the city itself, but from time to time attempts were made to ban those just outside the gates: in 1580, the mayor complained to the Lord Chancellor that

> . . .the players of plays . . . and tumblers [acrobats] and such like were a very superfluous sort of men . . . that the exercise of the plays was not only a great hindrance to the service of God but also a great corruption of youth with unchaste and wicked manners [and] the occasion of many frays, quarrels and other disorders within the city. (*Remembrancia, City of London*, quoted in A.L. Rowse, *The England of Elizabeth*, 1950)

The Council would not support a general ban on players at the theatre and inns, though – as they pointed out to the mayor, the Queen enjoyed having performances at court, and the actors needed to practise!

*This famous London cutpurse, John Selman, was active at the end of the Tudor period. He was finally caught on Christmas Day 1611 stealing from people in King James I's Royal Chapel. Soon afterwards he was hanged.*

### LONDON CUTPURSES SET UP THEIR VICTIMS

People visiting London were warned to look after their money. This is part of one cautionary tale.

> A roguing mate, and such another with him, were got upon a stall singing of ballads . . . very many gathered about to hear it, and divers buying [song-copies] . . . drew to their purses and paid the singers for them. The sly mate and his fellows, who were dispersed among them that stood to hear the songs, well noted where every man that bought put up his purse again, and to such as would not buy, counterfeit [false] warning was sundry times given by the rogue and his associate, to beware of the cutpurse, and look to their purses, which made them often feel where their purses were, either in sleeve, hose or at girdle, to know whether they were safe or no. (Robert Greene, *The Third and Last Part of Cony-Catching*, 1592)

You can imagine what happened to the purses . . . . However, these particular rogues were caught and, says the writer, "I hear of their journey westward [towards Tyburn, where the gallows stood] but not of their return". Why were thieves of this type called "cutpurses" at this time? (Look at the picture for a clue.)

Where might visitors to London today have to be especially careful of their purses or wallets?

CONFRONTATION, 1592

An investigation into a riot in London in 1592 put some of the blame on the officers of the Marshalsea prison, whose arrest of a culprit sparked off the trouble.

**. . . I am informed by the inhabitants of Southwark, men of best reputation** amongst them, that the Knight Marshal's men in their serving of their warrants do not use themselves in that good discretion and moderate usage as were meet to be done in like cases, but after a most rough and violent manner provoking [people] by such hard dealing to contend with [fight] them which otherwise would obey . . . as I understand they did in this case, where they entered the house . . . with a dagger drawn, affrighting the good wife who sat by the fire with a young infant in her arms, and afterwards, having taken the party and certain others and committed them to prison . . . these mutinous apprentices assembled themselves in their disordered manner; the said Marshal's men, being within the Marshalsea, issued forth with their daggers drawn and with bastinadoes [sticks] in their hands beating the people, whereof some came that way by chance but to gaze as the manner is, and afterwards drew their swords, whereby the tumult was rather incensed [worsened] and themselves endangered . . .(quoted in A.V. Judges, *The Elizabethan Underworld*, 1930)

Make a list of complaints against the behaviour of these law-enforcement officers.

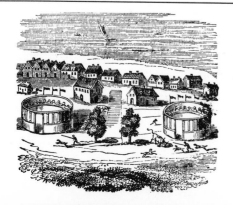

◁ *This view of London's South Bank in the 1560s shows the bull- and bear-baiting theatres, where animals were attacked by dogs (can you spot the bull being baited just outside one of the "theatres" or rings?). There were often rowdy scenes at these brutal shows. Have you ever heard the expression "like a bear-garden" used today?*

# Troublesome Apprentices

Many young men in the towns were apprenticed to craftsmen or merchants (girls, too, learnt crafts such as dressmaking in this way, but most girl apprentices were trained as domestic servants). The length of an apprenticeship was usually seven years. Masters were supposed to keep their apprentices in order but, as you can imagine, it was difficult to prevent fights between rival gangs, or the playing of forbidden games. Moreover, apprentices were only too ready to join in if any trouble broke out.

## THE PERFECT APPRENTICE

He must not lie forth of his master's doors [sleep out], he must not occupy any stock of his own [trade on his own behalf], nor marry without his master's licence [consent], and he must do all servile offices about the house and be obedient to all his master's commandments, and shall suffer such correction as his master shall think meet [fit]. (Sir Thomas Smith, *De Republica Anglorum*, 1583)

Do you think you would have liked to be an apprentice in Tudor times? What sort of jobs still require apprenticeships today?

## BANBURY'S APPRENTICES UP TO NO GOOD

**Banbury Council Order, 1563**
No innholder, victualler or any other man or woman shall receive or suffer to come within their houses any man's apprentice or child there to play at any unlawful games or other ways to spend

## STIRRING UP THE 'PRENTICES

In London, especially, apprentices were only too ready to seize the nearest club and join a fight. One such incident is here reported to Lord Burghley:

Upon the same Wednesday at night two companions, one being a tailor and the other a clerk . . . fell out . . . and the tailor raised the prentices and other light [irresponsible] persons and, thinking that the clerk was run into Lyon's Inn, came to the house with three hundred at the least, brake down the windows of the house, and struck at the gentlemen . . . (Recorder Fleetwood to Burghley, 18 June 1584, quoted in J. Dover Wilson, *Life in Shakespeare's England*, 1944)

The usual way to rouse local apprentices was to cry out "Clubs". (Look at page 10 for an example of this.) Why do you think apprentices were so keen to join in a fight?

their masters' or parents' goods or to receive of them any kind of ware for their expenses or victuals [food] on pain of 6s 8d and to have two days of imprisonment . . . (J.S.W. Gibson and E.R.C. Brinkworth, eds., *Banbury Corporation Records: Tudor and Stuart*, 1977)

How do some Banbury apprentices seem to have been paying for their food and amusements at local inns?

## A PROMISE OF GOOD BEHAVIOUR

Apprentices were supposed to obey their master as they would their father – and a master was allowed to beat them if they did not. Sometimes a special agreement about what an apprentice could or could not do was put into his indentures (the bargain made at the start of the apprenticeship). John, in the following example, was bound apprentice in 1531 to the Mayor of Leicester, a baker.

> **. . . the said John does bind himself . . . to be true servant for those [seven] years, and that he shall not steal none of his master's goods, not by 6d a year, and that he shall not use no gaming [gambling], nor he shall not make no promise of wedlock except his master give him leave . . .** (Records of the Borough of Leicester, quoted in *English Historical Documents* series, Vol.V, 1485-1558)

Why might *this* young apprentice be particularly tempted to steal?

*In the pillory.*

## A LONDON APPRENTICE'S CRIME AND PUNISHMENT

> **1561, the 9th day of July was the pillory set up in Cheapside for a prentice that had conveyed [stolen] from his master the sum of __ pound, and had bought him new apparel [clothes], new shirt, doublet and hose, hat, purse, girdle, dagger, and boots, spurs, butt-hose and a scarf, and this new all, and this did hang up on the pillory . . .** (J.G. Nichols, ed., *Diary of Henry Machin 1550-1563*, Camden Society, 1848)

Henry Machin was a merchant-tailor of London. He did not know exactly how much the apprentice had stolen. Apprentices were supposed to dress very simply, in short blue gowns. Find a book showing Elizabethan costume and see how this one would have looked when dressed up.

Imagine you are an elderly merchant or craftsmen. Make up a speech to a friend about your thoroughly bad apprentice.

# Sheep-Stealing

As most Tudor people lived in the country and made their living from farming, the stealing of animals was taken very seriously. A thief would face the death penalty if caught unless a sympathetic jury valued the animal at less than 1 shilling.

## SOLDIERS CAUGHT STEALING A SHEEP

In 1593 the town authorities at Southampton questioned some soldiers caught sheep-stealing. Notice the date – can you find out why there would be soldiers on the coast at that time? (The Date List on page 46 will help you.)

> 1593, February
> The Confession of William Banks, soldier, of __ Gloucestershire, serving man.
> He saith that the last night about 8 of the Clock in the evening he in company of 7 or 8 of his fellow soldiers whose names he doth not know, did go altogether out of the town . . . to a country house thinking to have stolen a hen, and when they were come to the gate the goodman bent a piece against [shot at] them, they not having done anything unto him at all . . . neither did he or his said fellow soldiers take any sheep or lambs whilst they were there . . . but thereupon presently returned . . . to the Town again.
> He farther saith that they went from thence unto a field next . . . the said house where they took up a sheep and there killed him and left the skin there, and brought him into the Town to . . . the sign of the Talbot . . . where the

## THIEVES IN SOMERSET

In 1596 country people in Somerset were suffering from the presence of groups of thieves in their county, as a local J.P. reported to Lord Burghley:

> . . . within these 3 months I took a thief that was executed this last assizes, that confessed unto me that he and two

*A watchful shepherd was needed to prevent sheep-stealing.*

> maid . . . let them in and there they dressed and boiled it and presently ate it up . . . (*Southampton Examinations and Depositions*, 1593)

Why would soldiers be tempted to steal, do you think? What kind of place was "the sign of the Talbot"?

**more lay [stayed] in an alehouse three weeks in which time they ate 20 fat sheep whereof they stole every night one . . .** (Edward Hext to Burghley, 25 September, 1596)

The writer went on to say that the most dangerous rogues in his area were "the wandering soldiers", who lived on stolen meat.

Notice the fate of the thief who was caught.

*Soldiers like this one became a problem to the authorities once they returned to England from foreign wars. Country people "lost" sheep and chickens when ex-soldiers passed through their areas on their way home from the coast.*

## CATCHING A SHEEP-STEALER IN KENT

When John Hunt of Sevenoaks in Kent lost two sheep in December 1596, he asked the borsholder [as the constable was called in Kent] to search local houses. The borsholder reported to the local J.P. (he calls himself "this deponent" in his account):

**. . . entering into the house of . . . Chaplen earlie in the morning, [we] found the said William Chaplen newly tumbled out of his bed betwixt his bed and the wall, then this deponent willed him to come forth, demanded of him whether he had any meat in his house and he answered no. Whereupon this deponent made search, in which time the said Chaplen broke through the wall of his house (being a simple cottage) and ran away and some of this deponent's company spying him, ran after him, felled him, and brought him back. And after . . . this deponent making searches . . . caused the wife of the said Chaplen to rise from the place where she sat and underneath her he found a pail and therein two loins of mutton, one breast, one shoulder, and one leg. And the said Chaplen being asked . . . where he had the same mutton he answered that his wife brought it in but when he knew not and his wife being demanded where she had it, she said that she found it under a hedge not far from her house in a bag.** (Information against William Chaplen, quoted in E. Melling, ed., *Kentish Sources: Crime and Punishment*, 1964)

Do you find Mrs Chaplen's explanation convincing? Notice the "simple cottage" in which the Chaplens lived. Do you know what it would have been built of, or can you work this out?

# Beggars and Vagabonds

There was sympathy in Tudor England for helpless people forced to beg to keep alive. Even before laws were passed – the most important was in 1601 – making payment of a "poor rate" or tax to help the poor compulsory, most towns had their own schemes. However, there was no help for those described by William Harrison in *Description of England* (1587) as the "thriftless poor . . . the rioter that hath consumed all, the vagabond that will abide nowhere". Such people were looked on as responsible for their own poverty, and they were punished – sometimes by being sent to a House of Correction, where they were given hard work to do.

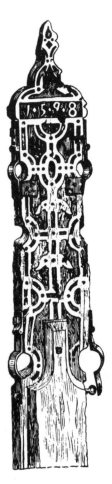

Beggars 'punished by the whip' were tied to whipping-posts like this one from Essex (you can read the date when it was put up at the top of the post).

### CHESTER COUNCIL RESTRICTS BEGGING, 1539

Forasmuch as by reason of the great number of multitude of valiant idle persons and vagabonds which be strong and able to serve and labour for their livings, and yet daily go on begging within the same city . . . it is ordained . . . that the number and names of all . . . needy mendicant people [beggars] shall be searched . . . and every of them assigned to what ward they shall resort and beg within the said city . . . and their names to be written in a bill and set up in every man's house within every ward for knowledge to whom they shall give their alms and to no other. And if any other person or persons come to any man or woman's door . . . to beg . . . then the same man or woman to give unto the same beggar no manner alms or relief but rather to bring or send him to the stocks within the same ward, or else to deliver him to the constable . . . and he to put him in the stocks, there to remain by the space of a day and a night . . . (Regulations Made At Chester as to Beggars, 1539, quoted in Bland, Brown and Tawney, eds., *English Economic History*, 1914)

Anyone who ignored this order was to be fined 1 shilling.

## PUNISHMENTS FOR BEGGARS IN NORWICH, 1571

... no person or persons old or young shall be suffered to go abroad [in the streets] after a general warning given, or be found a-begging in the streets at the sermon [at the time of a church service] or at any man's door or at any place within the city, on pain of six stripes with a whip.

At the house called the Normans ... shall be appointed a working place ... to set twelve persons or more upon work, which persons shall be kept as prisoners to work for meat and drink for the space of twenty and one days at the least, and longer if cause serve, and they shall not eat but as they can earn ... such persons ... shall be such as be able to work and daily notwithstanding will not work but rather beg, or be without master or husband, or else be vagabond or loiterers. Which persons shall begin their works at five of the clock in summer and shall end their works at eight ... and in winter to begin at six ... and to end at seven ... or half an hour past, with the allowance of one half hour or more to eat and a quarter of an hour to spend in prayer.

... And those that shall refuse to do their works ... to be punished by the whip ... (Quoted in E.M. Leonard, *Early History of English Poor Relief*, 1900)

Notice that girls old enough to leave home were expected to have either a master or a husband. Norwich called this House of Correction the "Bridewell", after the House of Correction set up in London.

## DISLIKE OF THE HOUSE OF CORRECTION

A Somerset J.P. (whose views on vagabonds you can discover on page 11) wrote in the 1590s:

I sent divers [various] wandering suspicious persons to the House of Correction: and all in general would beseech me to send them rather to the gaol ... they would not be sent to the House of Correction, where they should be forced to work. (Edward Hext to Burghley, September 1596)

Re-read the regulations from the Norwich House of Correction: are you surprised that some people preferred prison?

Can you think why town authorities and local J.P.s were so alarmed by unemployed people who wandered from place to place?

*Any wanderers, including musicians, risked being punished as vagabonds and put in the stocks.*

# Footpads and Highway Robbers

There were many dangers to face on Tudor roads. Travellers tried to walk or ride with a companion or a group, but even that was risky, as you will see from the extracts.

## ROBBERY ON BLACKHEATH

Blackheath near London was a favourite place for highway robbers. Today it is a pleasant open space, but in the sixteenth century it was wild and lonely. The following story tells of an old man returning from selling farm produce in London.

> ... as he was coming homeward on Blackheath, at the end thereof next to Shooters Hill, he overtook two rufflers, the one mannerly waiting on the other, as [if] one had been the master, and the other the man or servant, carrying his master's cloak. This old man was very glad that he might have their company over the hill, because that day he had made a good market; for he had seven shillings in his purse .... Thus, after salutations had, this master ruffler entered into communication with this simple old man, who, riding softly beside them, commoned [talked] of many matters. Thus feeding this old man with pleasant talk, until they were on the top of the hill, where these rufflers might well behold the coast about them clear, quickly steps unto this poor man, and taketh hold of his horse bridle, and leadeth him into the wood, and demandeth of him what and how much money he had in his purse ... ("Caveat for Conies" reprinted in A.V. Judges, ed., *Elizabethan Underworld*)

Why did the thieves wait until they reached the top of the hill before they attacked?

## A STOLEN PURSE

The Mayor of Southampton heard an accusation by a victim of an attack on a local road in December, 1592:

> Nicholas Reynolds, of Hill in the County of S'hampton, Millstone maker ... saith before Mr Mayor ... that upon Thursday night last between the hours of 6 and 7 of the clock in the evening, he ... going towards Hill about the watering pond, there met him two men who took from him his purse and in the same 25/7d and fleed from him, the one

Robbery on the highway was a very serious matter. Those robbers who were caught ended on the gallows.

32

drawing a sword at him and struck him and the other taking his purse from him. And he certainly knoweth . . . them for that by the moonshine he knew them . . . (*Southampton Books of Examinations and Depositions*, 6 December 1592)

What was the only form of light on the road on that winter's evening?

## DANGEROUS PLACES TO STAY

William Harrison warned travellers to beware of plots to rob them made at the inns where they slept overnight. The inn servants

. . . feel at their alighting whether their capcases [purses] or budgets be of any weight or not, by taking them down from their saddles, or otherwise see their store [money] in drawing of their

*A traveller drinking in an inn could find himself robbed next day by his drinking companions.*

purses, [and] do by-and-by give intimation to some . . . attendant daily in the yard or house, or dwellling hard by . . . whether the prey be worth the following or no . . . then the gentleman peradventure [perhaps] is asked which way he travelleth, and whether it please him to have another guest to bear him company at supper, who rideth the same way in the morning that he doth . . . . And often it is seen that the new guest shall be robbed with the old, only to colour out the matter and keep him from suspicion. Sometimes when they know which way the passenger travelleth, they will either go before and lie in wait for him, or else come galloping apace after . . . (William Harrison, *Description of England*, 1587)

If you like acting you could use these stories to make up scenes showing plots to rob Tudor travellers. You can find some scenes by Shakespeare, too, on this topic – look at his play *Henry IV, Part I.*

# Cheats and Confidence-Tricksters

You may have come across modern examples of people making money from cheating others – perhaps you have seen some of the television programmes that warn the public about individuals or companies that will take their money and give nothing in exchange. There were plenty of cheats in Tudor England, too, and books of stories about their various tricks were published.

William Harrison described some ways in which money could be gained from soft-hearted members of the public by unscrupulous rogues:

> . . . another sort . . . more sturdy than the rest . . . having sound and perfect limbs, do yet notwithstanding sometime counterfeit the possession of all sorts of diseases. Divers time in their apparel [clothes] also they will be like serving men or labourers: oftentimes they can play the mariners, and seek for ships which they never lost . . . they have devised a language among themselves which they name "Canting", but others [call] 'pedlers' French, a speech . . . of English and a great number of odd words of their own devising, without all order or reason, and yet such it is a none but themselves are able to understand . . . (*Description of England*, 1587)

Why would it be useful for these fake beggars to have a private language? (You might try making one up with your friends.)

*This "Abraham man" was a beggar who pretended to be mad in order to get sympathy – and money.*

## A FAMILY OF CONFIDENCE-TRICKSTERS

In 1591 the J.P.s of Staffordshire were sent a petition from 20 outraged inhabitants of Wheaton Aston:

> **Whereas there is inhabiting and dwelling in the said Town of Aston a simple and very innocent woman one Margery Lee and having in her house some small goods . . . the said Robert Russell and his wife perceiving and knowing her said simplicity, intending to make a prey of her promised to help her to a good marriage if that she would give them a featherbed and a pair of sheets who being thus allured thereunto consented . . .**

**34**

And whereas also when we with our wives and others of our households . . . are at Church to hear divine service then the said Russell's wife repaireth unto our houses unto such simple housekeepers as we shall happen to leave at home whom she enticeth and allureth to sell unto her loaves of bread . . . or any other things . . . promising to send them money therefore by a daughter . . . and that she shall put the same into a flower pot in the window [and saying] the money was left and that some naughty body had taken it . . .
(*Staffordshire Quarter Sessions Rolls II,* Roll 28)

The J.P.s ordered all three Russells to give security (that is, to deposit some money) to keep the peace, or else go to prison. Why did the Russells choose the time of church service to go round the houses "buying" provisions?

The Elizabethan author of *Caveat for Common Cursitors* included descriptions of female as well as of male cheats:

### A Demander for Glimmer
These demanders for glimmer be for the most part women; for glimmer, in their language, is fire. These go with feigned [pretended] licences [giving permission to beg] . . . having the hands and seals of such gentlemen as dwelleth near to the place where they feign themselves to have been burnt, and their goods consumed with fire. They will most lamentably demand your charity, and will quickly shed salt tears . . . . They will never beg in that shire where their losses [as they say] was . . .

Why would a "demander for glimmer" take care not to beg in the area where her home was supposed to have been burnt down?

## A CHEAT MEETS HIS MATCH

The cheats did not always win. One Londoner at least got the better of a cheating coalman, who tried to give her less than she had paid for (a favourite trick was to put dust or very small coal at the bottom of a sack; another was to use sacks with false bottoms which seemed to hold more than they did).

A cook's wife bargained with the collier and bought his coals . . . which being done, he carried the coals into the house . . . . And when the wife saw them, and perceiving there was scarce five bushels for eight, she calls a little girl to her, and bade her go for the constable; 'For thou cozening [cheating] rogue', quoth she, speaking to the collier, 'I will teach thee how thou shalt cozen me with thy false sacks, whatsoever thou dost to others, and I will have thee before my Lord Mayor.' With that she caught a spit in her hand and swore if he offered to stir she would therewith broach [stick it into] him . . .
Quoted in A.V. Judges, *The Elizabethan Underworld,* 1930)

The cheating coalman was only too glad to give the woman coal, sacks and all, for nothing, in exchange for being allowed to run away.

See if you can find out how much a bushel is in modern measurements; you probably already know what a spit was, and why no one would move if someone was threatening to use it as a weapon!

# Punishments

Punishments in this period were often brutal. They were also very public. Many people must have witnessed an execution and most would have seen minor offenders sitting in the stocks or standing in the pillory in their village or town.

## COMMON PUNISHMENTS IN THE 1580s

**Perjury [telling lies when under oath in a law-court] is punished by the pillory, burning in the forehead with the letter P .... Many trespasses also are punished by the cutting off of one or both ears from the head of the offender, [such] as the utterance of seditious words against the magistrates, fraymakers, petty robbers, etc. ... Rogues and vagabonds are often stocked and whipped; scolds are ducked upon cucking-stools in the water ...** (William Harrison, *Description of England,* 1587)

You can find out more about scolds and cucking-stools on page 41.

## ENDING ON THE GALLOWS

A large number of crimes were punishable by hanging. These included stealing anything worth more than a shilling. A career of crime could be expected to end with a death sentence, as the author of *Caveat for Common Cursitors* stressed.

**An upright-man ... must be next placed [described] .... These, not minding [caring] to get their living with the sweat of their face ... will wander, after their wicked manner, through the most shires of this realm .... Yea, not without punishment by stocks, whippings, and imprisonment, in most of these places .... Yet,**

*A common punishment was a beating "at the cart's tail". The victim was tied to a cart and was beaten as he followed the cart round the town.*

**notwithstanding, they have so good liking in their lewd, lecherous loiterings, that full quickly all their punishments is forgotten. And repentance is never thought upon until they climb three trees with a ladder.**

The "three trees" refers to a triangular-shaped gallows. The "upright men" were those who started by begging but went on to thieving, always pretending to be looking for work or else to be wounded soldiers.

One way of getting a lighter punishment for a crime was by claiming "benefit of clergy". This had once meant that you really were a Christian clergyman, but by the sixteenth century it was possible to claim "benefit of clergy" if you could show that you could read (though a good many Tudor people could *not* read, the days when only the clergy could do so were long past). For more serious crimes, though, "benefit of clergy" was not allowed, as you can see from William Harrison's account of penalties for theft:

> Thieves that are saved by their books and clergy, for the first offence, if they have stolen nothing else but oxen, sheep, money or such like, which be no open robberies, as by the highway side, or assailing [attacking] of any man's house in the night . . . are burned in the left hand, upon the brawn of the thumb, with a hot iron, so that, if they be apprehended again that mark betrayeth them . . . whereby they are sure at that time to have no mercy . . .

Why would it be worth even being branded in this way rather than receiving the usual punishment for theft?

There was a simpler way of avoiding severe punishment, which is often recorded by Tudor law-courts:

**Staffordshire Quarter Sessions, Easter 1590**
**Ric. Stanley late of Greeteyate labourer, Wm. Pollard of the same labourer and Ann his wife, Wm. Tofte late of the town of Stafford labourer, and Robt. Grundye late of Gratewich labourer; to answer touching certain felonies [serious crimes] and other misdeeds and offences.**
**Ret: Ric. Stanley and the rest have not been found . . .** (*Staffordshire Quarter Sessions Roll*, Easter 1590)

Although the men mentioned were outlawed – which meant having their property confiscated – for not appearing at the Autumn Quarter Sessions they made the right choice – felons were hanged.

*It seems strange to us today that people in Tudor times were punished for having different religious views from those approved by the ruler and Parliament. This picture shows a Protestant, Bishop Hooper of Gloucester, being burnt at the stake in Mary Tudor's reign.*

# Prisons

Tudor prisons were unhealthy places, whether they were small lock-ups or large castles. Prisoners often died of some kind of "fever". When, for example, an epidemic struck Brecon gaol in Wales in 1587 there were 39 deaths. All prisoners had to pay the gaoler for their keep.

## FEES IN READING PRISON, 1552

Assigned to John Reade, Serjeant, Keeper of the Gaol . . . of every person arrested . . . and . . . committed to the gaol, called the Grate, 6d.
And that every person attached [arrested] for debt . . . if the debt be under the sum of 6/8, he to pay for his fee 6d, and if the debt be 6/8 and above 8d . . . (Reading Records, *Diary of the Corporation*, Vol. 1, 1892)

*This prisoner is wearing leg-irons. Find out from the extracts what a rich man could do to escape having to wear them.*

The rich could buy privileges, but the poor starved or depended on charity. Cries of "One penny or half-penny, for Christ his sake, to buy some bread, to buy some bread!" could be heard through prison gratings.

## A FAVOURED PRISONER IN NEWGATE

Edward Underhill was imprisoned in 1553, in Queen Mary's reign, for writing an anti-Catholic ballad. At Newgate prison in London he was soon shown the ropes by an old acquaintance.

> . . . After supper, this good fellow . . . procured me to have a bed in his chamber . . .
> 'Sir!' said he . . . 'I will show you the nature and manner of them [the keeper and his wife], for I have been here a good while. They both do love music very well; wherefore you with your lute, and I to play with you on my rebeck [violin], will please them greatly. He loveth to be merry, and to drink wine; and she also. If you will bestow upon them every dinner and supper a quart of wine, and some music you shall be their white son, and have all the favour that they can show you!' And so it came to pass . . .
> When that I had been there about two weeks . . . I was cast into an extreme burning ague [fever], that I could take no rest, and desired to change my lodging. And so did, from one to another, but none could I abide; there was so many evil savours [smells] and so much noise of prisoners . . .
> During all the time of my sickness, I was constrained to pay 8d every meal; and as much for my wife, and for every friend that came to see me . . . and paid

**NEWE GATE**

*London's Newgate Prison, where Edward Underhill was sent, was part of one of the gates of the city.*

## HELP FOR POOR PRISONERS

Some wealthy people left money in their wills to help feed poor prisoners. John Stow's list of gifts made by Ralph Rokeby, a rich lawyer, in his will of 1596 tells us the names of some of the 14 or so prisons in London:

> . . . to the prisoners in the two compters [prisons] in London two hundred pounds, to the prisoners in the Fleet one hundred pounds, to the prisoners in Ludgate one hundred pounds, to the prisoners in Newgate one hundred pounds, to the prisoners in the King's Bench one hundred pounds, to the prisoners in the Marshalsea one hundred pounds, to the prisoners in the White Lion twenty pounds . . . (John Stow, *The Survey of London*, 1598)

These were quite considerable sums of money in 1596.

## A CRUEL GAOLER

Sometimes a keeper of a prison went too far in mistreating his charges, as John Stow in his *Survey of London*, published in 1598, recorded:

> Richard Husband . . . keeper of this compter in Bread Street, being a wilful and headstrong man, dealt, for his own advantage, hard with the prisoners under his charge . . . whereupon, in the year 1550 . . . he was sent to the gaol of Newgate, for the cruel handling of his prisoners; and it was commanded to the keeper to set . . . irons on his legs . . . and being released . . . he continued as afore . . .

> also 40s for a fine for irons [for not being chained] . . . (A.F. Pollard, ed., *Tudor Tracts*, 1903)

Edward Underhill had influential friends and was released after a month's imprisonment. Notice that his wife was allowed to join him in prison. This was not unusual in the case of gentlemen prisoners. What other things can you spot in the account which show he was treated leniently? What signs are there of harsh conditions for other prisoners?

Richard Husband never reformed, and because he owned the prison-house he could not be turned out. In 1555, the City of London built a new "compter" in Wood Street and moved all the Bread Street prisoners there.

Use the material on these pages to write a pamphlet attacking the prison system in Tudor England.

# Quarrelsome Neighbours

Small offences, and especially disputes between inhabitants, were dealt with by manorial courts in country districts (in the larger towns the mayor's court dealt with them). These courts were usually supervised by a servant of the Lord of the Manor. Villagers acted as a jury.

## COMPLAINTS AGAINST AN ESSEX MAN, 1592

At the court of Roger Harlackenden esquire of his manor of Earls Colne, 1592.

Henry Abbott junior hath drawn blood upon William Clerke and utterly hath maimed and lamed his finger.

In the night time he hath in his shirt come out of his house and in the street hath disquieted the watchmen.

Being commanded by the constables to ward [prison] the next day he refused.

He hath railed upon divers of his honest neighbours and them in most gross terms and speeches greatly abused.

Divers and sundry times heretofore he hath played at cards, dice, tables [backgammon] and other unlawful games and that very often.

He is very much given to contention [argument] and moveth great strife and variance between his neighbours . . .

(Quoted in F.G. Emmison, *Elizabethan Life: Home, Work and Land*)

Henry Abbott was fined the large sum of £5, and also reported to the Assize judges, who normally only dealt with very serious cases. Why do you think his neighbours found Abbott so annoying?

## A REAL FIREBRAND

Stock, Essex, 1574

Margery, wife of John James brawled and scolded with Roger Veale the lord's bailliff . . . and made an assault upon him in the constable's presence with firebrands . . . the constable to punish her upon the cucking-stool, to be dipped in water in the pond. (Quoted in F.G. Emmison, *Elizabethan Life: Home, Work and Land*)

Where would Margery James have found her pieces of burning wood? The bailiff's duty was to collect rents and fines. Perhaps this was what Margery James was angry about.

As well as the cucking- (ducking-) stool, Stock used a tumbril to punish scolds. This was a dungcart, and the offender was carried round the village in it.

## ACCUSATIONS

Bad quarrels between neighbours might lead to so much suspicion and ill-feeling that one party might accuse the other of witchcraft. Any piece of bad luck might seem part of a witch's revenge. In 1570 in Essex a farmer, accusing a neighbour's wife, explained that he

. . . having a sheep-shearing about this time and not inviting her thereto, being his neighbour, she, as he supposed, bewitched two of his sheep; for immediately after they were taken with sickness. (Quoted in Keith Thomas, *Religion and the Decline of Magic*, 1971)

An accusation like this was very serious – anyone convicted of witchcraft was executed.

Why do you think a villager would be disappointed not to be asked to a sheep-shearing? (Remember what was usually done to celebrate any kind of "harvest".)

## MISCHIEF-MAKERS IN YORKSHIRE

The court of the Manor of Acomb, on the outskirts of York, fined scolds. As you will see, other activities were also regarded as likely to provoke trouble in the village and punished accordingly.

**22 April, 1577**
**Penalties [to be imposed if the offence was repeated]:**
**Eliz. Banke not to chide or scold with her neighbours and to keep her house in the night season and not be an easinge droper [eavesdropper] under mens' windows        5.0d**
**11 April, 1583**
**Presentments [prosecutions]:**

**Agnes Vesseye, wife of John Vesseye, for that she did stand as an easinge droper at the window of Robt. Howse to hear what was said or done        6d**
(Acomb Court Rolls, *Yorkshire Archaeological Society Record Series*, 1969)

Notice that the fine Agnes actually paid is not nearly as high as the amount Elizabeth was threatened with if she did not stop her activities. The threat seems to have been successful, as she was not complained of again.

*A seventeenth-century woodcut, showing a "scold" or quarrelsome woman being ducked. Compare this ducking-stool with the one in the photograph on page 5.*

# Fights and "Unlawful Games"

There was a lot of brawling in the streets of Tudor England. Fights could easily start at an inn or ale-house – one reason why the authorities tried to limit the number of these establishments. Certain games were forbidden because they led to quarrels and fighting.

## FINES FOR FIGHTING IN YORKSHIRE

The Manor Court Records for Acomb tell us about one fight in 1568:

> **14 October 1568**
> **Presentments [prosecutions]:**
> **William Wright of Rufforth for drawing blood of Henry Bynks at Holgate    6s 8d**
> **Thomas Wright of Rufforth for drawing blood of John Cogell at Holgate    6s 8d**
> **John Cogell of Bikarton for drawing blood of Robert Holgate, constable of Holgate    6s 8d**

The fine for "drawing blood" was higher than the fine for fighting, which was usually 3s 4d. How many men were involved in this scuffle?

## "KEEPING THE PEACE" IN ABINGDON, BERKSHIRE

3 June 1556

> <u>An Order for clubs to be had in every Freeman's house</u>
> . . . it is . . . ordered that every inhabitant within this Borough shall forthwith and with all speed convenient prepare and have in readiness a good and sufficient club for the conservation of . . . peace, the same always to remain in the shops of every inhabitant or some other convenient place next adjoining to the street . . . (Bromley Challenor,ed., *Selections from the Records of the Borough of Abingdon*, 1898)

Would this arrangement have any disadvantages? (Remember that it was a cry of "Clubs!" that was used to call for help from the apprentices in London and other towns).

*Card games often led to cheating and to fights. How does this picture make fun of those foolish enough to get involved in card games with strangers?*

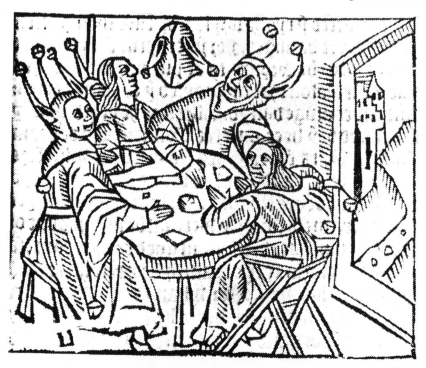

## TOO MANY WEAPONS

William Harrison commented on the number of people in Elizabethan England who carried weapons:

> Seldom shall you see any of my countrymen above eighteen or twenty years old to go without a dagger at the least at his back or by his side . . . . Our nobility wear commonly swords or rapiers with their daggers, as doth every common serving-man also that followeth his lord and master. Some desperate cutters we have in like sort, which carry two daggers or two rapiers in a sheath always about them, wherewith in every drunken fray they are known to work much mischief . . .
> (*Description of England*, 1587)

See if you can find out what a rapier was.

## TROUBLE OVER DICE AND CARD GAMES

Games of cards and dice usually involved betting. There were many opportunities for cheating.

> . . . there is seldom any playing at dice, but thereat is vehement chiding and brawling, horrible oaths, cruel, and sometimes mortal, menaces. I omit strokes, which now and then do happen . . . (Sir Thomas Elyot, *The Governor*, 1531)

"Cony-catchers" made a living out of cheating at cards. One Welshman who lost money in this way in London tried to fight back:

> . . . they . . . fleeced him of every penny that he had, and of his sword, at last the man smoked [suspected] them, and drew his dagger upon them at Ludgate . . . and would have stabbed one of them for his money. People came and stopped him, and the rather because they could not understand him . . .
> (Robert Greene, *A Notable Discovery of Cozenages*, 1591)

## A "MURDERING PRACTICE"

See if you can guess what dangerous game is being described here:

> . . . it may rather be called a friendly kind of fight than a play or recreation: a murdering practice, rather than a fellowly sport or pastime. For doth not everyone lie in wait for his adversary, seeking to overthrow him and to pick [pitch] him on his nose, though it be upon hard stones? In ditch or dale, in valley or hill, or what place soever it be, he careth not so he have him down . . . . So by this means sometimes their necks are broken, sometimes their backs, sometimes their legs, sometimes their arms . . .(Philip Stubbes, *The Anatomie of Abuses*, 1583)

This was Tudor football, "wherein is nothing but beastly fury and extreme violence", wrote Sir Thomas Elyot in *The Book Named the Governor*, (1531) advising that children should never be allowed to play the game. People were actually killed playing football: there were deaths in Essex games in 1567, in 1582 (twice) and in 1583.

Try to make up a story about a Tudor fight. You will find a good example of what such fighting could lead to in Shakespeare's play *Romeo and Juliet*. Look at Act III, Scene 1.

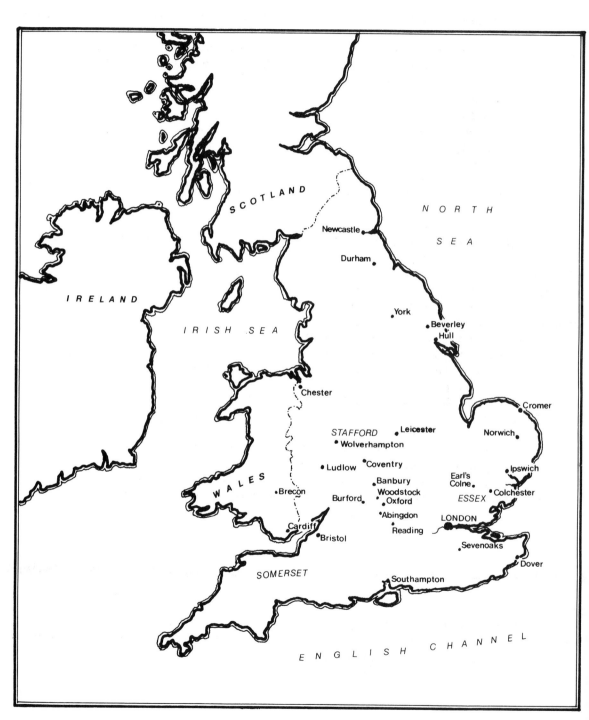

SCOTLAND

NORTH SEA

IRELAND

IRISH SEA

Newcastle

Durham

York

Beverley
Hull

Chester

Cromer

STAFFORD
Leicester

Norwich

Wolverhampton

Ludlow
Coventry

Ipswich

WALES

Banbury

Earl's
Colne

Colchester

Brecon

Burford
Woodstock
Oxford

ESSEX

Abingdon

LONDON

Cardiff

Reading

Bristol

Sevenoaks

Dover

SOMERSET

Southampton

ENGLISH CHANNEL

*N.B. Tudor rulers claimed Ireland as part of their kingdom, but they were still fighting for control there.*

# Difficult Words

| | |
|---|---|
| *Ascension Day* | the day that Christians believe Christ went up to Heaven: the sixth Thursday after Easter. |
| *Assizes, Assize Court* | law-courts held in local areas by royal judges to try serious crimes. |
| *buckler* | a small shield; "to play at the bucklers" means to fence or play at sword-fighting. |
| *budgets* | money-bags or wallets. |
| *Cheape, Cheapeside* | the market area in London. |
| *compter, counter* | a prison. |
| *conies* | rabbits; also used for those deceived by cheats or "cony-catchers". |
| *curfew* | a set time by which people had to be in their houses. |
| *divers* | various. |
| *enclosures* | the fencing off of common land or of large, open fields. |
| *footpad* | a robber on a roadway who travels on foot. |
| *fray* | a fight or brawl. |
| *gaol* | prison. |
| *glimmer, a* | someone who begs for money with a story of his or her house having been burnt down. |
| *J.P., justice of the peace* | local magistrate appointed by the ruler. |
| *lights (of a window)* | small panes of glass. |
| *Michaelmas* | the feast of St Michael: 29 September. |
| *ordained, it is ordained* | ordered. |
| *Quarter Sessions* | law-courts held in local areas by J.P.s |
| *rail, to rail* | to call abuse at, to scold or quarrel. |
| *ruffler, a* | a robber who has been, or pretends to have been, a soldier. |
| *scold, a* | a quarrelsome person. |
| *sedition* | plotting or aiding treason or rebellion. |
| *Shrove Tuesday* | the day before the period of Lent (the 40 days before Easter) begins in the Christian churches. |
| *treason* | an attempt to kill a ruler or overthrow a government by force. |
| *tumblers* | acrobats. |
| *vagrant* | a homeless unemployed person, also called a vagabond. |
| *wardens of the Marches* | men appointed by the ruler to defend the border with Scotland. |

# Money

**Money**

There were 12 old pence (d.) in a shilling (s.) and 20 shillings in a pound (£). A shilling is equal to 5p.

Prices seem very low, but remember that wages were too. Don't compare prices with those of today, without looking at earnings then and now.

# Date List

1485 Henry Tudor won the Battle of Bosworth and became king, as Henry VII. This ended the "Wars of the Roses" – a period when rival families fought for the crown of England.

1509 Henry VII died and his son Henry VIII became king.

1534 Henry VIII broke away from the Roman Catholic church headed by the Pope. He punished those who remained loyal to the Pope.

1536 A serious rebellion, the "Pilgrimage of Grace", broke out in the North, partly over the changes in the church.

1547 Henry VIII died and his nine-year-old son became king as Edward VI. His advisers made England more and more Protestant.

1549 Rebellions broke out in Cornwall and Devon (partly over religious changes) and Kett led a rebellion in Norfolk (mainly over economic problems).

1553 When Edward VI died, the Duke of Northumberland tried to make his own Protestant daughter-in-law, Lady Jane Grey, Queen. However, most people supported Henry VIII's daughter Mary and she won the throne (Northumberland and Lady Jane were executed). Mary was Roman Catholic.

1554 Sir Thomas Wyatt led a rebellion in Kent over Mary's marriage to the King of Spain. The Protestant Princess Elizabeth was suspected of plotting with Wyatt against her sister Mary. She was put in the Tower of London but released after two months. Many Protestants were burnt for their beliefs.

1558 Elizabeth became Queen when Mary died. Soon she made the English Church Protestant again.

1568 Mary Queen of Scots, fled to England. She was a Roman Catholic and would be Queen if Elizabeth died.

1569 The Earls of Northumberland and Westmoreland led a rebellion in the North in favour of returning to a Roman Catholic church.

1570 The Pope declared that Elizabeth was deposed as Queen of England. After this, Catholics in England were often suspected of plotting and were persecuted. Many were executed.

1572 The Duke of Norfolk was executed for plotting with Mary Queen of Scots.

1586 The Babington plot (to make Mary Queen of Scots, Queen of England) was discovered.

1587 Mary Queen of Scots was executed.

1588 The Spanish Armada, sent to invade England, was defeated.

1590s War with Spain continued.

1601 The Earl of Essex was executed for defying the Queen and attempting a rising in London.

1603 Elizabeth died and the Tudor period ended.

# Biographical Notes

ELYOT, Sir Thomas, born about 1490, died 1546, was a West country gentleman and a government servant under Henry VIII. His book *The Book Named the Governor* gave gentlemen advice on how to educate their sons.

HOLINSHED, Raphael, died in or about 1580 (his date of birth is not known). He came to London early in Elizabeth I's reign and produced two volumes of a history of England up to 1575 – the *Chronicles of England*.

HARRISON, William, born 1535, died 1593, was a clergyman who wrote a *Description of Britain* and a *Description of England*. These give much useful information about life in Elizabethan England.

LAMBARDE, William, born in 1536, died 1601,

was a J.P. in Kent. He was made Keeper of the Records (documents) in the Tower of London in 1601. In 1581 he published a handbook for J.P.s called *Eirenarcha*. He described the law courts of his day in another book, *Archeion*.

SMITH, Sir Thomas, born 1513, died 1577, was a scholar and a statesman. In 1571 he helped to enquire into the plotting of the Duke of Norfolk. He wrote an account of the government of Tudor England which was published in 1583 – *De Republica*.

STOW, John, born about 1525, died 1605, was a London tailor. He was very interested in the history of the City of London and wrote *The Survey of London* which was first published in 1598.

# Book List

### FOR YOUNGER READERS

Clarke, Amanda *Growing Up in Elizabethan Times*, Batsford, 1980

Harrison, Molly and Bryant, Margaret, *Picture Source Book for Social History: Sixteenth Century*, Allen & Unwin, 1951, reprinted 1968

Hart, Roger, *English Life in Tudor Times*, Wayland, 1972

### FOR OLDER READERS

Aydelotte, Frank, *Elizabethan Rogues and Vagabonds*, O.U.P., 1913, reprinted 1967

Dodd, A.H., *Life in Elizabethan England*, Batsford, 1961

Fletcher, Anthony, *Tudor Rebellions*, Longmans, 1968

Judges, A.V. (ed.), *The Elizabethan Underworld*, Routledge 1930, reprinted 1965.

Salgado, Gamini, *Elizabethan Underworld*, Dent, 1977

Williams, Penry, *Life in Tudor England*, Batsford, 1964

# Places to Visit

The Tower of London

Local museums: e.g. the City of Oxford museum has relics of the old prison where Tudor martyrs for their religion were kept; Ipswich museum has an old ducking (or cucking) stool.

Tudor buildings: e.g. the Guildhall in Lavenham, Suffolk, built in 1525 and sometimes used as a prison as well as a town-hall.

Older buildings used as prisons in Tudor times: e.g. the castles in Ludlow, Shropshire, and Dover, Kent; and buildings where local manorial courts were held, like Long Crendon court house in Buckinghamshire and Hawkshead court house in Cumbria.

Keep your eyes open too as you travel about the country for old stocks like those at Woodstock in Oxfordshire, shown below.

*These stocks are in Woodstock, Oxfordshire (remember that they had no roof over them when they were in use and not just a tourist attraction). If you are puzzled by the odd number of holes, look at the picture on page 16 and you will see why this did not matter.*

# Index

*(Numbers in italic indicate pages on which illustrations occur.)*